The B2B Sales Guide

Ashraf Abu Elayyan

Copyright © 2023 Ashraf Abu Elayyan
All rights reserved.
ISBN: **979-8373119290**

TABLE OF CONTENTS

Contents

Introduction 1
Chapter 1 2
The Importance of B2B Sales and the Role of the Salesperson .. 2
   1.1 The Value of B2B Sales for Businesses and the Economy 3
   1.2 The Key Responsibilities and Challenges of a B2B Salesperson 4
   1.3 The Qualities and Skills That Make a Successful B2B Salesperson 9
Chapter 2 15
Understanding Your Customers and Their Needs 15
   2.1 The Importance of Customer Research and Discovery 16
   2.2 Techniques for Identifying and Understanding Customer Pain Points 17
   2.3 Strategies for Building Trust and Rapport with Your Customers 22
Chapter 3 29
Developing a Strong Sales Pitch and Presentation 29
   3.1 Elements of a Successful Sales Pitch 29
   3.2 Crafting a Compelling Message that Resonates 35
   3.3 Strategies for Delivering a Confident and Persuasive Presentation 39
Chapter 4 43
Closing the Deal – Negotiation Tactics and Strategies 43

4.1 The Importance of Negotiation in B2B Sales..................44

4.2 Tips for Preparing for a Negotiation 48

4.3 Finalizing the Agreement and Sealing the Deal 53

Chapter 5 57

Building and Managing a Sales Pipeline 57

5.1 What Is a Sales Pipeline and Why It Matters 58

5.2 The Stages of a Sales Pipeline 59

5.3 Best Practices for Managing a Sales Pipeline 63

5.4 Common Sales Pipeline Mistakes to Avoid 68

Final Thoughts 71

The Heart of B2B Sales...71

The B2B Sales Guide

ABOUT THE AUTHOR

Ashraf Abu Elayyan is an award-winning author, recognized by Book Authority for writing one of the 'Best B2B Books of All Time.' He is a trusted advisor and mentor in B2B sales and digital transformation, with over 15 years of experience guiding businesses across the MENA region. Ashraf has partnered with leading organizations to drive growth, forge strategic alliances, and implement cutting-edge technology solutions.

Recognized as a go-to resource in B2B sales within the tech industry, Ashraf is also dedicated to mentoring the next generation of sales leaders. Realizing that true success comes from understanding clients' needs rather than simply pitching products, he developed what he now calls Smart Selling—a philosophy that prioritizes empathy, relationship building, and long-term value.

Introduction

Sales, in the end, is all about people. It's not just about what you're offering; it's about how you make the other person feel. In B2B sales, this truth becomes even more powerful. You're working with professionals who have their own challenges, goals, and pressures. When you take the time to really listen, to understand their world, something remarkable happens: you earn their trust. And trust, as you'll discover, is the most valuable currency in any business relationship.

Think back to a time when someone really listened to you. How did it make you feel? Probably respected, understood, and more open to their ideas. That's the kind of relationship you want to create with your clients. B2B sales isn't about flashy presentations or clever techniques. It's about showing up as someone who genuinely cares about helping the other person succeed.

This book isn't just a guide to selling—it's a guide to understanding people. When you approach every interaction with the mindset of helping rather than selling, you naturally build connections. You move from being just another salesperson to being someone who clients turn to for advice and solutions.

Chapter 1

The Importance of B2B Sales and the Role of the Salesperson

In B2B sales, it's easy to get lost in numbers, features, and bottom lines. But at the heart of every deal, there's something much more important: people. Every business you sell to is made up of individuals with their own challenges, pressures, and goals. When you really take the time to understand what's going on with those people, something magical happens. You stop being just another salesperson, and you start becoming someone they can trust.

Let's face it, most people don't like being sold to. They want someone who listens, someone who genuinely cares about what they need. That's where your role as a B2B salesperson comes in. It's correct you are offering a product or a service — but most importantly you're offering a solution to their problems, a way to make their lives and their businesses better.

The truth is, when you approach B2B sales with empathy and a willingness to help, you're no longer just chasing deals. You're building relationships that can last for years, even decades. That's the real value in what you do.

1.1 The Value of B2B Sales for Businesses and the Economy

Every business, no matter what it does, depends on other businesses to survive. It's easy to overlook, but think about it: the software you use, the office supplies on your desk, even the coffee you drink—it all comes from another business. That's the beauty of B2B sales. It's not just about selling a product; it's about keeping businesses running and helping them thrive.

When you work in B2B sales, you're doing more than closing deals. You're connecting companies with the things they need to grow, be more efficient, or solve a problem that's been holding them back. And that's not just important for the business you're selling to—it has a ripple effect. When one business grows, it creates more opportunities for everyone in its network.

Think about it like this: If you help a manufacturing company get the right software to streamline their operations, that company might grow faster. They'll need more materials, more workers, maybe even more space. Your sale isn't just a transaction—it's the start of something bigger.

And it doesn't stop there. B2B sales help drive innovation.

When companies invest in new technologies or services, they push industries forward. They experiment, they improve, and they find new ways of doing things. And when you're part of that, you're helping shape the future of entire industries.

At the end of the day, B2B sales aren't just about hitting quotas or closing deals. It's about making a real impact—on businesses, on industries, and even on the economy as a whole. When you think about it that way, the role you play as a B2B salesperson is a pretty big deal.

1.2 The Key Responsibilities and Challenges of a B2B Salesperson

Being a B2B salesperson means you're much more than someone who just pushes a product. You're someone who people rely on to help them solve real problems. It's a job that requires you to wear many hats—sometimes you're a problem solver, other times you're a consultant, and occasionally, you're even a therapist for your clients, helping them work through their business headaches. But it's a rewarding role, and when done right, it's one that makes a real impact. That said, it comes with a unique set of challenges that, once you understand, can make the job easier to navigate.

1. **Building Relationships That Matter:**

In B2B sales, your success often boils down to the relationships you build. You're not just selling to a business; you're selling to people. And people, by nature, are more likely to buy from someone they trust. Trust isn't something you can build with one good presentation or a single phone call. It's the result of consistently showing up, offering value, and being genuinely interested in the other person's success.

But here's the catch: relationships take time. A lot of time. You're not going to walk into a meeting, nail a pitch, and walk out with a deal. Most businesses want to take their time, weigh their options, and get multiple opinions before making a decision. It's not uncommon for several people to be involved in the buying decision, from the finance team to the head of operations. Each person has their own set of concerns, and it's your job to address them all.

So how do you build these lasting relationships? Start by being patient. Your focus shouldn't be on closing the deal as fast as possible, but rather on understanding what the client really needs and how you can help. Ask questions. Lots of them. And don't just listen to the answers—take notes, follow up on points they bring up, and show them you're paying attention to their specific situation. When you show you're invested in them as people, not just as a sale, you build trust. And in B2B, trust is everything.

2. Understanding What Really Matters to Your Client

Every client is different, and that means no two sales are the same. While your product or service might be a great solution for one company, it might not hit the mark for another in the same way. That's why one of the most important skills in B2B sales is the ability to truly understand your client's unique challenges. It's not enough to know what your product does — you need to know *how* it fits into their world and *why* it makes sense for their business.

This means going beyond surface-level conversations. Sure, they might tell you what they need on the first call, but you need to dig deeper. Ask questions that help you get to the heart of their challenges. What's the real problem they're trying to solve? What's the impact on their business if they don't find a solution? And what's their biggest fear when it comes to making a buying decision?

The challenge is that sometimes, clients don't even fully understand their own needs. They might know they have a problem, but they haven't figured out the root cause yet. This is where you step in as a consultant.

Your job isn't just to sell a product — it's to help them see the bigger picture and identify what they really need. By being curious and genuinely interested in helping them, you'll find that you can offer a solution that truly makes a difference in their business.

3. Dealing with the Long Haul

One of the biggest differences between B2B and B2C sales is the timeline. In consumer sales, someone might decide to buy a product in a matter of minutes, but in B2B, the process is much longer. A sale can take weeks, months, or even years to finalize. And while that can be frustrating, it's also an opportunity.

The long sales cycle means you have time to really get to know your client and their business. It gives you the space to build trust, offer value and become an indispensable partner in their decisions. But it also means you need to stay organized and keep the momentum going without being overbearing.

The challenge is keeping up your own energy and motivation when things move slowly. There will be times when you feel like you're spinning your wheels—meeting after meeting without making any headway. It's easy to lose patience or get discouraged. That's why having a system in place to track your progress and manage your pipeline is essential. You need to know where each client stands, what their concerns are, and what the next step should be. That way, even if the process feels slow, you know you're moving in the right direction.

Staying engaged with your prospects is key. You don't want to disappear for weeks at a time and hope they'll remember you when they're ready to make a decision. Keep in touch and share useful insights or industry news, and always be ready to provide additional information when they need it. It's about striking that balance between staying top-of-mind without being pushy.

4. 4. Bouncing Back from Rejection

No matter how good you are at building relationships, understanding your client's needs, and managing a long sales cycle, rejection is part of the game. Not every deal will close. Sometimes it's because the client went in a different direction, and other times it's simply out of your control—budgets get cut, priorities shift, and sometimes the timing just isn't right. And let's be honest: rejection stings. After investing weeks or even months into a deal, hearing a "no" can feel like a punch to the gut.

But here's the truth: rejection isn't the end. It's part of the journey. The best salespeople don't let rejection define them—they let it refine them. Every time you lose a deal, it's an opportunity to learn. Ask yourself what could you have done differently? Was there a concern you didn't address? Did you miss a cue that things were heading in the wrong direction?

The key is resilience. You have to be able to pick yourself up, dust yourself off, and get back out there. Sales is a numbers game, and every "no" brings you one step closer to a "yes." Stay focused on the bigger picture and remember that rejection is just one part of the process.

1.3 The Qualities and Skills That Make a Successful B2B Salesperson

Success in B2B sales isn't about having a perfect pitch or being able to recite product specs by heart. It's about who you are, how you interact with people, and the mindset you bring to every conversation. The most successful B2B salespeople aren't always the ones with the loudest voices or the most aggressive tactics—they're the ones who understand people, who listen more than they talk, and who are always willing to go the extra mile for their clients.

Let's talk about the qualities and skills that make the difference in B2B sales. These are the things that set apart the people who close deals and those who build lasting relationships.

1. Strong Communication and Listening Skills

It might sound obvious, but the best salespeople are

incredible communicators. And no, that doesn't just mean they can give a killer presentation. It means they know how to make a real connection with someone. They know how to explain complex ideas in simple terms, how to get their point across without overwhelming the client, and—most importantly—how to listen.

Because here's the thing: real communication starts with listening. In sales, you're often in a room with decision-makers who are dealing with a million different things. The more you listen and really tune in to what's being said (and what isn't being said), the better you'll understand their concerns, fears, and goals. And once you understand that, your job becomes much easier. You're not just selling a product—you're offering the exact solution they need because you've taken the time to really hear what they're asking for.

2. Empathy and Understanding

Great salespeople know how to put themselves in their client's shoes. It's not just about understanding the technical needs of the business; it's about understanding the human side of things. How is this decision going to impact the person you're talking to? What pressures are they under? What keeps them up at night?

Empathy allows you to connect on a deeper level with your

client. When you genuinely care about what they're going through, it shows. You're not just pushing your product—you're offering a solution to make their life easier. And when clients feel like you get them, they trust you. That trust is what opens the door to deeper conversations, larger deals, and long-term partnerships.

Empathy isn't something you can fake. It comes from genuinely caring about your client's success. And that's what separates the good salespeople from the great ones.

3. Resilience and Perseverance

Let's face it—sales is hard. You're going to hear "no" more often than "yes," and you're going to hit walls that seem impossible to break through. But the best salespeople know that setbacks are temporary. They don't let rejection derail them. Instead, they see it as part of the process, something that can be learned from and used to refine their approach.

In B2B sales, perseverance is key. You might spend months working on a deal, and just when you think everything's going smoothly, something changes. Maybe the client's budget gets cut, or a decision-maker gets cold feet. It's frustrating, but it's also part of the job. The ability to bounce back from these setbacks and keep pushing forward is what keeps successful salespeople moving. They don't give up at the first sign of trouble — they adjust, adapt, and keep going.

This resilience doesn't just apply to the big picture; it's needed on a day-to-day level. Following up with leads, keeping clients engaged, and staying organized in the long sales cycle can wear anyone down. But those who can persevere through the daily grind come out on top.

4. Adaptability and Problem-Solving

No two sales situations are the same. Every client has different needs, concerns, and goals, which means you have to be able to adapt your approach to fit each unique situation. The best salespeople are those who can think on their feet. They're problem-solvers at heart, constantly looking for new ways to meet their client's needs.

Adaptability means being flexible in how you present your solution. It might be about finding a new angle or offering a customized approach that fits exactly what the client is looking for. It could even mean reshaping the deal entirely to accommodate budget constraints or internal challenges the client is facing. Sales isn't one-size-fits-all, and the more you can tailor your strategy to meet the specific needs of each client, the more successful you'll be.

And let's be real: in sales, things rarely go according to plan. Deals fall through, clients change their minds, and unexpected problems pop up. The ability to stay calm, shift gears, and find a way forward is what makes the best salespeople stand out.

5. Patience and Long-Term Thinking

B2B sales is a long game. It's not about quick wins—it's about playing the long-term strategy. The best salespeople know that success doesn't always come right away. It's about building relationships over time, staying patient when deals take longer than expected, and focusing on the bigger picture.

Patience is critical when you're navigating long sales cycles or working with clients who need time to make decisions. Rushing the process rarely works, and it often backfires. Instead, successful salespeople focus on providing value throughout the journey. They stay in touch, offer support, and build trust, knowing that when the timing is right, the deal will come together.

This long-term thinking also applies to the way they view their relationships with clients. Great salespeople aren't just looking to close one deal—they're thinking about the partnership that can grow from that first sale. They know that a happy client will keep coming back, and the effort they put in today will pay off down the road.

6. Organization and Time Management

In B2B sales, you're juggling a lot—multiple clients, long

sales cycles, follow-up emails, presentations, and proposals. Without strong organizational skills, things can quickly slip through the cracks. The best salespeople are those who stay on top of their workload, managing their time effectively and making sure they're always a step ahead.

Having a system in place—whether it's a CRM, a planner, or just a detailed to-do list—keeps everything running smoothly. Organization isn't just about keeping track of tasks; it's about managing your relationships, staying engaged with prospects, and making sure that no opportunity is missed. When you're organized, you can stay focused on what really matters—building connections and closing deals.

These qualities and skills may sound like a lot to take on, but they're all learnable. The more you practice them the more natural it becomes. And the more you lean into these qualities, the more you'll find that B2B sales is about so much more than selling—it's about connecting, helping, and building something that last

Chapter 2

Understanding Your Customers and Their Needs

At the heart of every successful B2B sale is a simple truth: you can't sell effectively if you don't understand your customer. It's not enough to know what product you're offering—you need to know how that product fits into your customer's world, what problems it solves for them, and why they should care.

Understanding your customer isn't just about gathering facts or ticking boxes on a checklist. It's about getting to the root of what they truly need, even when they might not be able to fully articulate it themselves. And the better you understand your customer, the better equipped you are to offer a solution that feels like it was custom-made for them.

2.1 The Importance of Customer Research and Discovery

Think of customer research as your foundation. Without it, you're just guessing. And in B2B sales, guessing isn't a strategy—it's a gamble. When you take the time to really dig into who your customer is and what they need, you're setting yourself up for success before you even have that first meeting.

Customer research is about more than knowing the basics, like the company's size or industry. It's about understanding their goals, their challenges and how your product or service can make a difference in their day-to-day operations. It's also about knowing who you're speaking to—each person in the buying process has their own concerns, so knowing whether you're talking to the decision-maker or an influencer matters.

Start by looking at the company's history. What's their story? How have they evolved, and where are they trying to go next? The more you understand where they've been and where they're headed, the more you can tailor your approach to fit their narrative.

But research doesn't stop at gathering information. Discovery is where you start to uncover the deeper layers. This is where your conversations with the client come into play. Ask thoughtful questions, and listen carefully to what's being said—and what's not being said. Often, the real needs are just below the surface, and it's your job to find them.

Why is this so important? Because when you truly understand your customer, you can connect the dots for them. You're no longer just presenting a product—you're offering a solution to a problem they've been struggling with. And that changes everything. Suddenly, the conversation shifts from "Why should we buy this?" to "How soon can we get started?"

Good research and discovery do more than prepare you for a meeting. They build your confidence, give you insights that can help steer the conversation and position you as someone who knows exactly what the customer is dealing with. That's when you stop being just another salesperson and start becoming a trusted advisor.

2.2 Techniques for Identifying and Understanding Customer Pain Points

If you want to truly connect with a customer and offer them

something they can't resist, you need to get to the heart of their pain points. What are they struggling with? What's keeping them up at night? In B2B sales, you're not just offering a product—you're solving a problem. And the better you understand that problem, the more valuable you become.

But here's the thing: customers don't always tell you what their pain points are upfront. Sometimes they don't even know how to articulate them clearly. That's where your skills as a salesperson come into play. You need to ask the right questions, pay attention to the clues, and dig a little deeper to uncover what's really bothering them.

Let's look at some techniques to help you identify and understand those pain points:

1. Ask Open-Ended Questions

When you're talking to a potential customer, don't just ask yes or no questions. Open-ended questions invite them to share more about their situation. Instead of asking, "Are you looking for a solution to [X] problem?", try something like, "What are the biggest challenges your team is facing right now?" or "Tell me about your goals for this year."

Open-ended questions get people talking, and the more they talk, the more you learn. It's in those detailed answers where you'll often find the real issues they're dealing with—the kind that your product or service can solve.

2. Listen to Their Language

Pay close attention to the words and phrases your customer uses when describing their situation. Are they talking about being overwhelmed, lacking time, or feeling under-resourced? Are they mentioning frustration with current tools or processes? These words give you valuable insight into their emotional state and help you zero in on what's not working for them.

When you repeat their own language back to them, it shows you're paying attention and you get what they're going through. For example, if they say, "Our current software is slowing us down," you can follow up with, "So, it sounds like your team's productivity is being affected by the software. Let's talk about how we can speed that up."

3. Look for Patterns

If you've been in B2B sales for a while, you'll start to notice common problems that many companies face. Whether it's inefficiency, scalability issues, or trouble with customer retention, these patterns can help you spot potential pain points even before the customer brings them up.

Once you've identified these recurring themes, you can gently guide the conversation toward those topics. For example, "I've noticed that a lot of companies in your industry are struggling with scaling their operations. How are you managing growth right now?" This opens the door for the customer to share their own challenges, and you can step in with your solution.

4. Follow Up Regularly

Customer needs evolve, and pain points can shift over time. That's why it's important to stay in touch and keep asking questions. A pain point that wasn't a priority three months ago might suddenly be top of mind today. Following up gives you the chance to catch those changes and stay relevant in the conversation.

Even if you've had a productive first meeting, it's essential to keep checking in. A simple, "How are things going with [X issue]? Has anything changed since we last talked?" shows that you're invested in their success, not just in closing the deal.

5. Do Your Homework

Sometimes, you can spot potential pain points before you even speak to the customer. By doing thorough research on their company, industry, and competitors, you can make educated guesses about what they might be struggling with. Check out their website, read recent news about them, and look at what other companies in their space are doing.

Armed with this information, you can enter the conversation with insights that show you understand their world. For example, "I noticed your competitor recently launched a new product line. Has that affected your market share or created any new challenges for your team?" This kind of prep work helps you ask better questions and uncover pain points faster.

Finding and understanding customer pain points is all about curiosity and empathy. When you ask the right questions, really listen, and show that you're invested in solving their problems, you build trust. And once you've identified what's really causing them pain, you can offer a solution that's not just a good fit—it's exactly what they need.

2.3 Strategies for Building Trust and Rapport with Your Customers

No matter how great your product is, trust is the key to getting your customers on board. Without it, your pitch, your features, even your pricing won't matter. People buy from those they trust, and building that trust is a process that takes time, consistency, and genuine effort. Trust and rapport are the foundation of every successful B2B relationship. When customers believe in you—not just in what you're selling—they're more likely to choose your solution, and more importantly, stick with you in the long run.

Building trust isn't something that happens instantly. It's built piece by piece, over multiple interactions, with actions that reinforce your reliability and intent to help.
So, how do you build that kind of connection?

Let's break it down into some actionable strategies that go beyond the basics and dive into what really works.

1. Listen More Than You Talk

It sounds simple, but this is one of the most underrated skills in sales: just listen. When you're meeting with a customer, instead of jumping straight into your pitch, start by asking questions and listening carefully to their answers. And not just surface-level listening—really dig into what they're saying. What are their main concerns? What are the challenges they're facing day to day? What keeps coming up in their responses that signals something they might not even fully realize themselves?

When you make listening a priority, two things happen. First, you gather valuable information that helps you tailor your solution to exactly what they need. Second, and just as important, you show them that you value their perspective. People feel more connected and open when they know they're being heard. A good rule of thumb is to talk less than you listen, especially early on in the relationship. When the conversation feels more about them than it does about your product, you're already building trust.

And don't just listen to what they're saying—pay attention to how they're saying it. Are there underlying frustrations? Are they holding back concerns? Picking up on these cues can help you guide the conversation in a way that brings out the real issues they're facing.

2. Be Honest and Transparent, Even When It's Hard

Trust isn't built through perfection—it's built through honesty. If your product or service doesn't perfectly match the customer's needs, don't try to force it. Instead, be upfront about what your product can and can't do. Acknowledging limitations might seem risky, but here's the reality: people trust those who are transparent. No product is perfect, and customers know that. What they care about is whether you're someone they can rely on to give them the full picture.

Being honest, especially when it's not in your immediate favor, sets the stage for long-term trust. If a customer sees that you're willing to be candid about a potential drawback, they'll trust you even more when you highlight the strengths of your solution.

Also, be prepared to admit when you don't know something. If a customer asks a question you don't have an answer to, don't bluff. Say, "I'm not sure, but let me find out for you." Then follow through. This kind of transparency shows you're committed to getting things right rather than just pushing the sale.

3. Follow Through on Every Promise

Here's a basic but often overlooked truth: if you say you're going to do something, do it. Whether it's sending additional information, scheduling a demo, or following up with a proposal—your ability to keep your word is one of the strongest trust builders there is. And it's not just about the big things. Even the small promises matter. If you tell a client you'll send them a document by the end of the day, make sure it's in their inbox before they close their laptop.

It's these little actions that build your reputation over time. When customers see that you're reliable, they start to relax. They don't have to chase you for updates or worry about whether you'll follow through. They know you've got it under control.

This extends to timelines as well. If you know something's going to take longer than expected, communicate that right away. Managing expectations is crucial. People appreciate being kept in the loop, even if the news isn't exactly what they wanted to hear. It shows that you respect their time and are working to keep things on track.

4. Share Your Expertise Without Holding Back

In B2B sales, you're often working with people who look to you for answers—not just about your product, but about the industry, trends, and best practices. When you freely share your knowledge, you position yourself as a trusted expert. And the more you help them, the more they'll want to work with you.

Don't be afraid to offer advice beyond just what your product does. For example, if you know your client is struggling with a specific operational issue, share ideas or resources—even if they don't directly relate to your solution.

This kind of value-added input shows that you're thinking about their bigger picture, not just the immediate sale.

And remember, you're not just selling a product; you're selling your ability to help them solve problems. The more knowledgeable and helpful you are, the more likely they'll be to trust you as a partner in their success.

5. Be Responsive, But Don't Overwhelm

One of the fastest ways to erode trust is to disappear after the initial conversation. Customers want to feel like they can count on you—not just during the sale, but throughout the entire process. If they have a question or concern, respond quickly. Even if you don't have a full answer right away, a simple acknowledgment goes a long way. Something like, "I've received your message and I'm looking into it. I'll get back to you shortly," reassures them that you're on it.

That being said, don't bombard your clients with constant messages. Finding the right balance is key. If you're too pushy, it can come across as self-serving. The goal is to make sure they know you're there when they need you, without making them feel pressured. It's about being available, reliable, and respectful of their time.

6. Take a Genuine Interest in Their Success

It's easy to fall into the trap of thinking about your clients only in terms of the deal. But if you truly want to build rapport, you need to care about their success beyond the transaction. Ask about their long-term goals, their biggest challenges, and what they see for their business in the future.

When you show genuine interest in their overall success, not just the immediate sale, it changes the dynamic. You're no longer just a vendor—you're a partner who's invested in their growth. This could be as simple as following up after a sale to ask how things are going or sending over a useful resource that's not directly related to your product but could help them with their business goals.

Customers want to work with people who care, and showing that you're thinking about their success—even when there's nothing immediate in it for you—makes a lasting impact.

7. Be Patient and Let Trust Develop Over Time

Finally, remember that trust doesn't develop overnight. It's built gradually, through consistent, reliable actions. Be patient. Sometimes, building a relationship takes longer than expected, and that's okay. The key is to stay present, follow up, and continue offering value.

You may not close a deal on the first meeting, but the relationships you nurture over time will pay off. Trust is a long-term investment, and if you focus on helping rather than selling, you'll see the rewards down the line. B2B sales is about playing the long game, and when you're in it for the long haul, trust is your most powerful tool.

Building trust and rapport isn't a complicated formula, but it does require dedication, consistency, and a genuine desire to help. It's about showing up, doing what you say, and focusing on the customer's needs above all else. When you do that, the sales follow naturally.

Chapter 3

Developing a Strong Sales Pitch and Presentation

A sales pitch is not just about delivering information. It's about creating a moment—a moment where the customer suddenly sees things differently, where they realize that your solution is exactly what they've been looking for. The magic of a great pitch isn't in the product itself, but in the connection you create between the customer's problem and your solution.

Think about it: every decision-maker you talk to is bombarded with options, pitches, and promises. What makes your sales pitch stand out? It's not about overwhelming them with features or jargon. It's about speaking directly to their needs and show them that you understand their challenges and offering a way forward that feels clear and achievable.

3.1 Elements of a Successful Sales Pitch

When it comes to crafting a sales pitch, the temptation is always to dive into the details of your product or service. After all, you're proud of it. You know how it works inside and out, and you've seen firsthand the value it can bring. But here's the thing: your customer isn't interested in the shiny features or technical specs—not unless they can immediately see how it solves their problem.

A successful pitch isn't a list of everything your product does. It's a story. And in that story, the customer is the hero, not the product. Your job is to show how your solution fits into their world and helps them overcome the obstacles in their path and achieve their goals.

So, how do you do that?

1. Start with Their Problem, Not Your Product

Your pitch should always begin with the customer's pain points. What challenges are they facing? What are their biggest frustrations or obstacles? Before you dive into what your product can do, make sure they feel heard and understood. This shows that you've done your homework and that you're focused on helping them, not just making a sale.

When you start with their problem, you immediately shift the conversation to something they care about. For example, instead of opening with, *"Our solution offers X, Y, and Z features,"* try something like, *"We know that one of the biggest challenges companies like yours face is managing workflow efficiently while keeping costs down. Let's talk about how we can help you solve that problem."*

This approach gets their attention because it's about them, not you. It shows that you understand their needs and sets the stage for positioning your solution as the answer they've been searching for.

2. Focus on Benefits, Not Features

It's tempting to get into the details of what your product can do, but most customers aren't interested in the technical specs. They want to know *how* it's going to make their life easier, save them time, or help them achieve their goals. That's why your pitch should focus on benefits—what the customer gains—rather than features.

For example, if you're selling a software solution, don't just say, "Our product has an advanced analytics dashboard." Instead, explain the benefit: *"With our software's analytics dashboard, your team can get real-time insights that allow you to make faster, data-driven decisions, which ultimately boosts your team's productivity and improves your bottom line."*

By framing the conversation around benefits, you're speaking the customer's language. They care about the outcome, not the technical details, so make sure your pitch is about how your solution impacts them directly.

3. Tell a Story

People connect with stories far more than they connect with facts and figures. A great pitch should include a narrative that draws the customer in and makes your solution feel relevant to their world.

This could be a case study or an example of how you helped another company in a similar situation. It humanizes the pitch and makes it easier for the customer to envision themselves experiencing the same success. For example, *"We recently worked with a company similar to yours that was struggling with [specific problem]. After implementing our solution, they saw a 30% increase in efficiency within the first three months. I can see your team achieving the same, if not better, results."*

When you tell a story, it moves the conversation beyond the abstract and into something tangible and real. It's not just about selling a product—it's about showing the customer how your solution can change their business for the better.

4. Anticipate and Address Objections

Every customer has concerns, and part of crafting a successful pitch is addressing those concerns head-on. Don't shy away from potential objections—instead, weave answers into your presentation naturally. If you anticipate their questions or doubts, it shows that you're prepared and understand their situation.

For example, if you know budget is going to be a concern, you can say something like, *"I know budget is always a key consideration. That's why we offer flexible pricing options that can be tailored to fit within your specific financial goals without sacrificing quality or service."*

By tackling objections before they even voice them, you position yourself as a thoughtful partner who's already considering their concerns. This builds trust and makes them feel more confident in moving forward with you.

5. End with a Clear Call to Action

A great pitch always ends with a clear next step. Don't leave the conversation hanging in the air—guide them toward action. Whether it's scheduling a demo, arranging a follow-up meeting, or getting started with a trial, you need to close with a specific request.

For example, *"Based on everything we've discussed, I believe our solution is a great fit for your team. Let's schedule a time next week to walk through a live demo so you can see it in action. How does Tuesday afternoon work for you?"*

Making the next step clear and actionable helps you keep the momentum going and make it easy for the customer to say yes.

The elements of a successful pitch may seem simple, but when combined effectively, they create a powerful message that resonates with your customer.

Remember, your pitch isn't just about your product—it's

about how your product can make a real difference in their world. When you lead with their needs and focus on delivering value, you'll find that the conversation naturally moves toward a positive outcome.

3.2 Crafting a Compelling Message that Resonates

When you're building a sales pitch, it's easy to get caught up in trying to impress. Maybe you're tempted to show off every impressive feature or throw out a bunch of stats. But here's the truth: a great pitch isn't about impressing your customer—it's about *connecting* with them. It's about making your message land in a way that feels relevant, clear, and personal.

The reality is, people make decisions based on emotion first and logic second. Your customer is more likely to respond to a story that connects with their experience than a list of features that sound impressive but don't feel real to them. Crafting a message that resonates means speaking directly to their needs, challenges, and goals in a way that feels human, not robotic.

Here are some strategies to craft a message that sticks:

1. Speak Their Language

Every industry, every company, every customer has its own language. Whether it's specific jargon, a way of describing their challenges, or a tone that reflects their company culture, understanding how your customer speaks—and mirroring that in your pitch—goes a long way.

This isn't about being overly formal or trying to sound more technical than you need to. It's about making sure your words align with how your customer thinks. For example, if you're talking to someone in a startup, they might value speed and agility more than a large, established company that focuses on stability and long-term growth. Craft your message in a way that reflects their world. Use their terms, their concerns, and their way of thinking to create a message that feels familiar to them.

2. Focus on the Impact, Not the Features

You could have the most advanced product in the world, but if the customer can't see how it impacts them personally, it won't matter. The key to a compelling message is to focus on the outcome, not the features. What's going to change for them if they use your solution? How is their life going to be easier, faster, more profitable?

Instead of saying, *"Our software has real-time data analytics,"* try something like, *"With our software, you'll be able to make faster, data-driven decisions that save you time and give you a competitive edge."* It's not about what your product *is*—it's about what your product *does* for them. Show them the benefits that matter in their world, and you'll create a message that resonates.

3. Tell a Story They Can See Themselves In

We're wired to respond to stories. A good story sticks in our mind far longer than a bullet-pointed list ever will. When you're pitching, think of your message like a story where your customer is the main character. They have a challenge or a problem, and your solution is what helps them overcome it.

For example, instead of just explaining your product's capabilities, share a real-world example of how someone in a similar situation used your solution to solve a problem. It could be something like, *"We recently worked with a company like yours that was struggling to manage their growing client base. With our solution, they were able to streamline their operations and grow without needing to expand their team. I can see how this would work for you too."*

Stories are powerful because they help the customer see themselves using your solution. They make the abstract tangible and relatable, and that's when your message really hits home.

4. Be Clear and Concise

It's tempting to try to cover everything in your pitch, but less is often more. Keep your message clear and to the point. Don't overwhelm your customer with too much information—focus on the key points that matter most to them.

When your message is clear and concise, it's easier for your customer to absorb and understand. A cluttered message leads to confusion, and confused customers don't buy. So, simplify. Focus on the value you bring, and leave room for questions and conversation instead of flooding them with information they don't need right now.

5. Make It About Them

At the end of the day, your message should revolve around the customer, not you. This means shifting from "We offer..." or "Our product..." to phrases like, "You'll experience..." and "Your team will benefit from...". The more you can frame your pitch around how the customer will benefit, the more it will resonate with them.

By putting them at the center of your message, you show that you're thinking about their needs and how you can help. It turns the conversation from a sales pitch into a collaborative discussion about how you can support their goals.

A compelling message isn't just about sounding impressive—it's about creating a connection. When you speak the customer's language, focus on the impact, tell a relatable story, and keep things clear, you're crafting a message that resonates on a human level. And that's the kind of message that sticks.

3.3 Strategies for Delivering a Confident and Persuasive Presentation

You've got your pitch ready, but now comes the critical part—delivering it in a way that captures your audience's attention and keeps them engaged. Your presentation doesn't have to be perfect, but it does need to feel authentic, clear, and focused. This isn't about being the flashiest or having the slickest slides—it's about being real, confident, and making your customer feel like you *get* them.

The truth is, people respond to connection, not perfection.

They want to hear your story, see your passion and trust that you're someone who understands their challenges. So how do you deliver a presentation that's confident and leaves your audience eager to work with you?

Let's break it down.

Be Prepared, but Stay Flexible

Preparation is key. You need to know your material inside and out, but here's the trick: don't sound rehearsed. You want to be ready to talk naturally, like you're having a conversation, not reading off a script. Flexibility is just as important as preparation—your customer might take the conversation in a new direction, and that's okay. Be prepared to follow where the discussion goes, rather than sticking rigidly to a plan.

Instead of memorizing every word, focus on knowing the flow of your presentation. Understand the key points you want to hit and the value you're offering, but leave space for improvisation when needed. The goal is to sound knowledgeable and approachable, not like you're giving a lecture.

Capture Their Attention from the Start

First impressions are everything. You don't need a long introduction about yourself or your company—get straight to the point that matters to your customer. What's the challenge they're facing, and how can you help?

Start with a hook that pulls them in. Maybe it's a question that gets them thinking: *"What would it mean for your team if you could reduce your project timelines by 20%?"* Or it could be a bold statement about what's possible: *"Imagine saving hundreds of hours every quarter without increasing your headcount."* From the first sentence, you want them leaning in, eager to hear more.

Use Visuals to Support, Not Dominate

Visual aids can be powerful, but they should support your message, not overshadow it. Your slides shouldn't be crammed with text. Instead, use them to enhance what you're saying—a graph that illustrates a key point, a simple image that underscores a solution, or a case study result that helps tell your story.

Think of your visuals as the backup singers, not the star of the show. You want your audience focused on *you* and the value you're bringing, not reading slides while you talk. Keep it clean, clear, and relevant.

Make Eye Contact and Connect

There's a simple but powerful way to show confidence: eye contact. Whether you're pitching to one person or a full boardroom, making eye contact creates a sense of connection. It shows that you're present, engaged, and speaking directly to the people in front of you. And when people feel seen, they're more likely to trust you.

Engage your audience as you go. Ask them questions, get their input, and listen to their feedback. The more interactive your presentation, the more connected they'll feel to what you're saying. Don't just talk *at* them—bring them into the conversation.

Pace Yourself—Slow Down to Make an Impact

When you're nervous, it's easy to rush through a presentation. But here's a tip: slow down. A steady, confident pace gives your audience time to absorb what you're saying. It also shows that you're in control of the conversation.

Pause for effect after key points. Let your words sink in before you move on. And don't be afraid to leave room for silence—it can be a powerful tool in keeping your audience focused on what's important.

Be Ready for Questions—And Address Them Naturally

Questions are a sign that your audience is engaged, so don't shy away from them. In fact, anticipate them. If you know there's a common concern about pricing or implementation, weave it into your pitch before they even ask: *"I know budget is always a consideration. That's why we've developed flexible pricing options tailored to your specific needs."*

By addressing potential objections before they're raised, you show that you've thought things through and that you understand their concerns. It builds confidence and keeps the conversation flowing smoothly.

Close with Confidence and Clarity

When you get to the end of your pitch, don't let the energy fade. Your close is where you lock in the next step, so make it count. Be specific about what you want to happen next. Whether it's scheduling a follow-up meeting, setting up a demo, or starting a trial, your close should leave no doubt about the path forward.

Something like, *"I'm confident our solution is a great fit for your team. Let's set up a time next week to dive into a demo. How's Tuesday afternoon for you?"* Clear, direct, and confident. You're leading them toward action without being pushy.

Your presentation doesn't have to be perfect, but it does need to feel real. Confidence doesn't come from knowing all the answers—it comes from being authentic, listening to your customer, and focusing on how you can help them. When you're clear, connected and focused on delivering value, your audience won't just hear your message—they'll feel it.

Chapter 4

Closing the Deal – Negotiation Tactics and Strategies

For many, the word "negotiation" can feel intimidating, like a high-stakes game where one side wins and the other loses. But the truth is, great negotiations aren't battles, they're collaborations. Negotiations are more about finding a solution that works for both parties, where everyone walks away feeling satisfied.

The key to successful negotiation is simple: it's not about pushing your agenda; it's about understanding theirs. What does the customer really care about? What's non-negotiable for them? When you approach the conversation with a mindset of cooperation, not confrontation, you create an environment where both sides can win.

4.1 The Importance of Negotiation in B2B Sales

Let's be honest, negotiation isn't always easy, but it's a critical part of B2B sales. It's where the deal either comes together or falls apart. And the stakes are high.

But here's something to remember negotiation isn't about winning or losing. Negotiations are about building trust and finding common ground. Your goal isn't just to close this deal, it's to create a partnership that lasts.

In B2B, the negotiation process often involves more than just price. You might be discussing timelines, implementation details, payment terms, or ongoing support. The more complex the deal, the more factors there are to negotiate. That's why being prepared and knowing what matters most to your customer is essential.

Negotiation in B2B sales is less about haggling and more about finding a solution that works for both sides. When you approach it with that mindset, it changes the tone of the conversation. Instead of being about concessions and compromises, it becomes a discussion of how you can make the deal work in a way that's mutually beneficial.

Understand What's Really on the Table

Before you even step into a negotiation, it's crucial to understand what's at stake for both sides. Sure, price is often a major factor, but there's usually more going on under the surface. What's most important to the customer? Are they focused on getting the best price, or are they more concerned about delivery speed, ongoing support, or customization options?

By understanding their priorities, you can shape the conversation to address their key concerns. If price is a sticking point, maybe you can offer flexible payment terms. If they're worried about timelines, perhaps you can offer a faster implementation schedule in exchange for locking in the deal sooner. The point is, negotiation isn't just about numbers — it's about offering solutions that make sense for both sides.

Know Your Non-Negotiables

Just as important as understanding the customer's priorities is knowing your own. What are your non-negotiables? Where are you willing to be flexible, and where do you need to stand firm? Having a clear understanding of this going into the negotiation will help you stay focused and avoid agreeing to terms that don't make sense for your business.

For example, you might be willing to offer a discount for a long-term contract, but not for a one-off deal. Or maybe you can provide extra services if the customer agrees to a larger order size. Whatever your boundaries are, know them upfront so you're not caught off guard in the heat of the moment.

Keep the Conversation Collaborative

The best negotiations don't feel like power struggles. They feel like problem-solving sessions, where both parties are working together to find a solution that benefits everyone. When you approach negotiations with a spirit of collaboration, you lower the tension and create an environment where open dialogue can happen.

Instead of focusing on what you can "win," try shifting the conversation to what both sides can gain. For example: *"I understand that budget is a concern for your team. Let's explore how we can structure this deal in a way that works for both of us."*

By keeping the tone collaborative, you make the customer feel like they're part of the solution, not just someone being sold to. And that's how you build long-term partnerships.

Be Ready to Give and Take

Negotiation is rarely a straight line. There will be points where you'll need to compromise, but it's all about balance. If you're giving something up, make sure you're getting something in return. This give-and-take creates a sense of fairness and helps both sides feel like they're walking away with value.

For instance, if the customer is asking for a lower price, you might agree but ask for a longer contract term in return. Or if they need faster delivery, you can provide it if they're willing to cover additional costs. The key is to make sure that every concession you make is balanced by a gain that matters to your business.

Stay Calm and Confident

Negotiation can sometimes get heated, especially when there's a lot at stake. But here's the thing: the calmer and more confident you are, the more control you'll have over the conversation. If the customer senses panic or uncertainty, they may push harder for concessions.

Even if things aren't going the way you'd hoped, keep your cool. Remember, it's a process. If you've done your homework, you're in a strong position to navigate whatever comes up. And if you hit a roadblock, don't be afraid to suggest taking a break to regroup. Sometimes a little time away can give both sides the clarity they need to come back and find common ground.

Negotiation in B2B sales is less about closing the deal at any cost and more about creating a foundation for long-term success. It's about understanding what's really important to both sides, staying flexible, and working together to build a partnership that benefits everyone involved. The more you approach negotiation as a conversation rather than a contest, the more successful you'll be—not just in this deal, but in the many deals to come.

4.2 Tips for Preparing for a Negotiation

Negotiation success doesn't happen in the meeting room—it starts long before you sit down at the table. Preparation is the foundation of every strong negotiation. The more prepared you are, the more confident you'll feel, and the smoother the conversation will go. Think of preparation as your secret weapon. It's what allows you to stay calm, handle objections, and guide the discussion in a way that works for both sides.

So, how do you prepare effectively for a negotiation? Let's walk through a few key tips to help you enter that room ready for anything.

1. Know What You Want (and What You Can Live Without)

Before the negotiation even begins, be clear on what you want. What's your ideal outcome? What's your bottom line? Understanding your own goals is the first step to effective negotiation. But it's just as important to know where you can be flexible. What are the areas where you're willing to compromise, and what's absolutely non-negotiable?

For example, if your goal is to close a long-term deal, maybe you're willing to offer a discount in exchange for a longer contract commitment. Or, if pricing is firm, perhaps you can be flexible on delivery schedules or additional services. Having these boundaries in mind before the conversation starts helps you stay focused and ensures that you don't agree to something that doesn't make sense for your business.

2. Research the Customer's Priorities

Negotiation is a two-way street. It's not just about what you want — it's about understanding what the customer wants, too. Before stepping into the negotiation, do your homework. What are their main concerns? What's driving their decision-making process? Is it budget, timing, or maybe a specific feature of your solution? The more you know about their priorities, the more effectively you can position your offer to meet their needs.

If you've had previous conversations with the customer, revisit your notes. Look for patterns or recurring themes in what they've said. If not, try to gather as much information as possible about their business and industry. Being informed allows you to anticipate their concerns and address them head-on in the negotiation, which builds trust and keeps the conversation moving forward.

3. Anticipate Their Objections

One of the best ways to prepare for a negotiation is to think through the objections your customer might raise. What are their potential sticking points? Maybe it's the price, the timeline, or the implementation process. By anticipating these concerns ahead of time, you can come to the table with solutions already in mind.

For example, if you know the customer is going to be sensitive about pricing, you might prepare by offering flexible payment options or demonstrating how the long-term benefits outweigh the initial cost. Or, if they're worried about implementation, you could present a clear plan that shows how you'll support them throughout the process.

Being proactive about objections shows that you've thought through their concerns, and it helps you maintain control of the conversation.

4. Prepare Your Concessions Ahead of Time

In any negotiation, you're going to give up something. That's the nature of the process. The key is to plan your concessions strategically. What are you willing to offer in exchange for something of equal value? And just as importantly, how can you frame those concessions in a way that still benefits you?

For instance, if the customer asks for a discount, maybe you agree to lower the price slightly, but only if they commit to a larger order or extend the contract length. Or if they need faster delivery, you offer it in exchange for paying upfront. The idea is to make sure that every concession you make strengthens the overall deal for both sides.

Having these options ready before you go into the negotiation allows you to stay flexible while protecting your own interests.

5. Practice Your Pitch

Yes, negotiation is about back-and-forth conversation, but it's also about presenting your value clearly and confidently. Before you step into the negotiation, make sure you've practiced your pitch. You need to be able to communicate why your solution is the best fit for their needs, how it solves their problems, and why it's worth the investment.

Practicing your pitch ahead of time helps you refine your messaging and ensures that you can deliver it smoothly, even if the conversation takes an unexpected turn. It also gives you a chance to anticipate tough questions and work on framing your answers in a way that keeps the discussion moving forward.

6. Visualize the Outcome

This might sound simple, but it's powerful: take a moment to visualize the negotiation going well. Picture the conversation flowing smoothly, with both sides engaged and interested. Imagine the customer responding positively to your offer and reaching a mutually beneficial agreement. Visualizing success helps set a positive tone before you even start, and it can boost your confidence going into the meeting.

This mental preparation primes you to stay calm, confident, and focused on the best possible outcome, even if things get tense or complicated.

4.3 Finalizing the Agreement and Sealing the Deal

Negotiation isn't over until the agreement is signed and the deal is sealed. This final stage is where all the work you've put into the relationship, the pitch, and the back-and-forth negotiations comes together. But getting to that signature isn't just about presenting a contract—it's about making sure both sides feel confident, satisfied, and ready to move forward.

At this point, it's crucial to ensure clarity, alignment, and momentum. You don't want any loose ends or misunderstandings cropping up once the ink is dry. A smooth close means you not only secure the deal but also lay the groundwork for a long-term partnership.

Confirm the Details

Before you present the final agreement, take the time to confirm that everyone is on the same page. Walk through the key points of the deal and check that all terms and conditions have been addressed to the customer's satisfaction. This might include pricing, delivery timelines, support agreements, or any specific concessions made during the negotiation.

You don't want any surprises at the eleventh hour, so ask directly: *"Just to confirm, are we all aligned on these terms?"* This gives the customer a final opportunity to raise any lingering questions or concerns. The clearer everything is now, the fewer issues you'll have down the road.

Keep the Energy Positive

The finalization of a deal should feel like a win for both sides. Keep the energy positive and collaborative, even in the final stages. If the tone feels transactional or rushed, the customer might start second-guessing. But if they feel good about the partnership and excited about moving forward, they're much more likely to close the deal without hesitation.

So, instead of focusing only on the details, take a moment to talk about the bigger picture: *"I'm really excited about what we'll achieve together. This is just the beginning of a great partnership, and I'm confident this solution will have a big impact on your business."*

This keeps the conversation focused on the value you're bringing and reminds them why they're making this investment in the first place.

Make Signing the Agreement Easy

It's surprising how many deals get stalled at the final hurdle because of logistical issues with the contract. Once the customer is ready to sign, make the process as easy as possible. If they're ready to move forward, don't let paperwork or complex approval processes slow things down.

Use digital signing tools if possible, and ensure the contract is clear, concise, and easy to review. Eliminate any unnecessary steps or confusion so they can sign off without delay. The smoother the process, the faster you'll get the deal locked in.

Reinforce the Value Before Signing

Right before the contract is signed, it's a good idea to briefly reinforce the value of the deal. You don't need to repeat your entire pitch, but a quick reminder of what's being delivered and why it matters can solidify their confidence.

Something like: *"As we finalize this agreement, I just want to highlight how this solution is going to directly address the challenges we discussed. I'm confident that this will streamline your process and lead to measurable improvements within the first few months."*

By reinforcing the benefits one last time, you help eliminate any last-minute doubts and give them a clear reason to sign.

Be Ready to Address Last-Minute Concerns

Even at this stage, don't be surprised if a last-minute question or concern pops up. The customer might ask for clarification on a small point or even try to negotiate one final aspect of the deal. This is normal, and your job is to remain calm and handle it without derailing the momentum.

If a concern arises, listen carefully, address it directly, and steer the conversation back toward the close. Sometimes, it's as simple as answering a question or providing a bit of reassurance. The goal is to keep the process moving forward while maintaining the customer's confidence.

Set the Stage for What Comes Next

Once the deal is signed, your relationship with the customer doesn't end — it's just beginning. The way you close the deal sets the tone for everything that follows, so make sure you end on a positive and proactive note.

After the agreement is finalized, outline the next steps clearly: *"Now that we've got everything signed, here's what's going to happen next. We'll start with [the onboarding process, the implementation timeline, etc.], and I'll be your main point of contact throughout the process."*

This shows that you're thinking ahead and that you're committed to making the next phase as smooth as possible. It also reinforces the idea that this is a partnership, not just a one-time transaction.

Chapter 5
Building and Managing a Sales Pipeline

If you think of sales as a journey, then the sales pipeline is your map. It's what shows you where you are, where you're going, and how to get there. But building and managing a sales pipeline isn't just about filling it with as many leads as possible. It's about making sure each opportunity is carefully tracked, nurtured, and moved through the stages with intention.

A strong sales pipeline isn't a one-size-fits-all template. It's a dynamic process that needs constant attention, adaptation, and a clear understanding of where your potential customers are in their decision-making journey. If you don't have a handle on your pipeline, you're essentially flying blind.

5.1 What Is a Sales Pipeline and Why It Matters

Let's start with a question: Do you really know where your deals stand?

I'm not talking about a vague sense of "who's interested." I mean a crystal-clear picture of which prospects are about to convert, which are on the fence, and which ones need a little more time. That's what a sales pipeline gives you — clarity.

A sales pipeline is a visual snapshot of where each deal is in the sales process. It's not just a way to track leads; it's a way to measure progress, predict revenue, and prioritize your time. Without it, you're essentially guessing, hoping that something lands. With it, you're strategic, focused, and always a step ahead.

But a pipeline isn't just a static list of names. It's a dynamic system that shows you exactly where each prospect is, from the moment they show interest to the point they sign on the dotted line. And when you manage that pipeline effectively, you're in control of your sales process — you know what's working, what's not, and where to focus your efforts.

5.2 The Stages of a Sales Pipeline

Every pipeline has stages. Think of these stages as milestones in your customer's journey. Each stage represents a step closer to closing the deal. Here's how a typical sales pipeline might look, but remember, every business can (and should) tweak this to fit their specific process:

1. Lead Generation: Finding Potential Customers

This is the starting point—where you're generating leads and identifying potential customers. These are people who've shown interest in your product or service. Maybe they visited your website, downloaded an ebook, or attended a webinar. Whatever the source, they're on your radar.

But here's the trick: not every lead is equal. At this stage, your job isn't just to collect as many names as possible. It's about identifying leads that are worth your time. You don't need a hundred random names; you need a handful of the right ones.

2. Qualification: Sorting the Good from the Bad

Now that you've got some leads, it's time to qualify them. This stage is all about asking the right questions: *Is this prospect a good fit for what I'm offering?* Are they in the right industry? Do they have the budget? Are they decision-makers?

Think of this as a filtering process. You're sorting through your leads to find the ones that are worth pursuing. You're looking for signs that they have a real need, that they're ready to take action, and that your solution is a good fit for their problem. The more thorough you are here, the smoother the rest of the process will go.

At this stage, you might ask questions like:

- **Budget:** Do they have the financial resources to invest in your product or service?
- **Authority:** Are you speaking to the person who can make the final decision?
- **Need:** Is there a genuine problem that your product can solve?
- **Timeline:** Are they ready to move forward soon, or are they still in the research phase?

When you qualify leads effectively, you stop wasting time on people who aren't a good fit and start focusing on those who are.

3. Meeting/Presentation: Making Your Case

This is where things get serious. You've identified the lead, qualified them, and now it's time to show them what you can do. In this stage, you're delivering a presentation or a demo, explaining how your solution can solve their problem.

But here's the key: it's not about *you*; it's about *them*. Your pitch needs to be tailored to their specific challenges, showing them how your product will make their life easier or their business better. This is where you connect the dots between their pain points and your solution.

The best presentations don't feel like sales pitches. They feel like problem-solving conversations, where you're offering real value and helping them see the path forward.

4. Proposal: Putting the Deal on Paper

At this point, you've had the big conversations. Now, it's time to formalize the offer. In the proposal stage, you're outlining the terms, pricing, and details of what you're offering. This is where you lay everything out clearly, so the customer knows exactly what they're getting and how it will work.

The proposal is your chance to reinforce the value you bring. You're not just talking about cost; you're talking about return on investment. Make sure the proposal reflects everything you've discussed so far, and tailor it to their specific needs.

It's also important to make this process smooth. A confusing or overly complicated proposal can slow down the deal. Clarity is your best friend here.

5. Negotiation: Finding Common Ground

This is where the back-and-forth happens. Maybe they want a lower price, faster delivery, or additional services. Whatever the case, negotiation is all about finding a middle ground where both sides feel good about the deal.

Remember, negotiation isn't about winning or losing—it's about reaching an agreement that works for both parties. Keep the conversation collaborative. Be ready to give, but make sure you're getting something in return. The goal is to create a win-win situation where both sides feel they're walking away with value.

6. Closing: Sealing the Deal

This is the moment you've been working toward. The deal is ready to close, and both sides are aligned. At this stage, you're finalizing the contract, getting signatures, and locking in the agreement.

But don't rush. Make sure everything is clear and that there are no loose ends. You want both sides to feel confident about moving forward. Once the deal is closed, celebrate it—but also start thinking about the next steps, like implementation and follow-up.

7. Post-Sale: Building Long-Term Relationships

The sale might be closed, but the relationship is just beginning. The post-sale stage is about delivering on your promises and setting the foundation for a long-term partnership. Follow up, check in, and make sure they're getting the value they expected. Happy customers lead to repeat business and referrals, which feed right back into your pipeline.

5.3 Best Practices for Managing a Sales Pipeline

Managing a sales pipeline can feel like juggling—there are leads in different stages, deals at risk of stalling, and timelines that stretch across weeks or months. But with the right approach, you can turn that chaos into something organized and productive. The goal isn't just to keep the pipeline moving; it's to manage it with intention, so you always know where your deals stand and what your next move should be.

Here are some best practices that can help you stay on top of your sales pipeline and make sure it's always working for you:

1. Keep Your Pipeline Clean and Up to Date

A cluttered pipeline is a dangerous thing. When your pipeline is full of old or unqualified leads, it's hard to see where you should focus. Keep your pipeline clean by regularly reviewing and updating it. Remove leads that have gone cold, and focus on nurturing the ones that are still in play.

Think of it this way: your pipeline should be like a well-tuned engine. If it's full of outdated or irrelevant data, it's going to run inefficiently. By keeping it clean, you can see where your efforts are making the most impact, and that's what drives progress.

2. Prioritize High-Value Opportunities

In sales, time is one of your most valuable resources. That's why it's important to prioritize high-value opportunities—deals that have the highest potential to close and provide the greatest return. These are the leads you should spend the most time nurturing and moving through the pipeline.

To prioritize effectively, ask yourself these questions: Which deals are closest to closing? Which leads have shown the most interest? Which opportunities align best with your product or service? By focusing on the deals that are most likely to convert, you're using your time where it counts.

3. Stay in Touch with Your Prospects

One of the most common reasons deals fall apart is a lack of communication. Prospects get busy, things get delayed, and before you know it, a once-hot lead has gone cold. That's why regular, meaningful follow-ups are essential.

But follow-ups shouldn't feel robotic. They should be tailored and thoughtful. Maybe you send a useful article that's relevant to their industry or offer a quick check-in to see how things are progressing on their end. The goal is to stay top of mind without being pushy. The more value you provide during the follow-up process, the more likely the deal will keep moving forward.

4. Use Data

Your pipeline isn't just a way to track deals—it's a source of valuable data. By analyzing the patterns in your pipeline, you can make smarter decisions about where to focus your efforts. For example, if you notice a lot of deals are stalling at the negotiation stage, that could signal a need to refine your pricing strategy or address common objections earlier in the process.

Look at the data: How long are deals staying in each stage? Where are the most drop-offs happening? Which types of leads are converting most successfully? This kind of insight helps you identify bottlenecks and optimize your sales process.

5. Focus on Relationship-Building, Not Just Closing

In the rush to close deals, it's easy to forget that sales is about building relationships. Prospects aren't just names in your pipeline—they're real people with real needs. The more you focus on helping them succeed, the more naturally your pipeline will move.

Remember, every interaction is a chance to build trust. Whether it's during the initial outreach, the proposal stage, or after the sale is closed, your goal should always be to provide value and create a positive experience. When your prospects feel understood and supported, they're much more likely to stick with you—not just for this deal, but for future deals, too.

6. Set Clear Milestones

A sales pipeline can sometimes feel like a long journey with no clear end in sight. That's why it's important to set milestones and celebrate progress along the way. Maybe it's moving a deal to the next stage, getting a verbal commitment, or finalizing the terms of a proposal. These small wins are worth recognizing because they keep momentum going.

By breaking the process down into smaller steps, you also make it easier to stay focused. Instead of feeling overwhelmed by the distance between a cold lead and a closed deal, you can focus on moving one step forward at a time. And that progress adds up quickly.

7. Don't Be Afraid to Cut Your Losses

Not every lead is going to turn into a deal, and that's okay. One of the hardest but most important things you can do is recognize when it's time to let a lead go. If a prospect has been sitting in your pipeline for months with no movement, it's time to make a decision: either reignite the conversation or move on.

By cutting your losses early, you free up time and energy to focus on the opportunities that are still viable. It's a tough call, but it's part of managing your pipeline effectively. The more disciplined you are about this, the stronger your pipeline will be.

8. Always Be Ready to Adapt

Sales is never static. Markets change, customer needs evolve, and new competitors enter the scene. That means your pipeline should never be set in stone. Be ready to adapt to changes—whether it's adjusting your strategy for lead generation or tweaking how you qualify prospects.

The best salespeople are always learning and adjusting. By staying flexible and open to change, you ensure that your pipeline stays relevant and effective, no matter what shifts in the marketplace.

9. Keep Your Eye on the Big Picture

Managing a pipeline day-to-day can sometimes feel like getting lost in the weeds. But don't forget the bigger picture: your pipeline is about building sustainable, long-term growth. Every deal you close isn't just a one-off win—it's part of a larger strategy to drive consistent revenue and build lasting relationships.

Stay focused on the end goal: a healthy, well-managed pipeline that delivers reliable results, month after month.

5.4 Common Sales Pipeline Mistakes to Avoid

Even with the best intentions, it's easy to fall into some common traps when managing a sales pipeline. These mistakes can slow down progress, lead to missed opportunities, and create unnecessary frustration. Let's take a look at a few of the most frequent pipeline missteps—and how to avoid them.

Letting Leads Go Cold

The most common mistake is letting leads sit too long without any follow-up. Prospects don't stay warm forever. If you leave them hanging, they'll move on. The key to keeping your pipeline healthy is to stay engaged with your leads—always checking in, nurturing the relationship, and keeping the conversation going.

Avoid letting too much time pass between touchpoints. Set reminders in your CRM to follow up regularly. Even a simple "just checking in" email can keep a lead from going cold.

Focusing on Quantity Over Quality

It's tempting to think that a bigger pipeline means more sales. But if your pipeline is filled with unqualified or irrelevant leads, it becomes a distraction. Quality beats quantity every time.

Focus on the leads that have the highest potential to convert. This means being disciplined about qualifying leads early on, so you're not wasting time on people who aren't ready to buy.

Not Tracking the Right Metrics

If you're only focused on how many deals you're closing, you're missing a huge part of the picture. You also need to track the flow of your pipeline. How long does it take for leads to move from one stage to the next? Where are the bottlenecks?

Tracking the right metrics gives you insight into your sales process, allowing you to make adjustments and improve efficiency. Pay attention to metrics like average deal size, win rate, and the length of your sales cycle. These numbers tell a story—and if you're not tracking them, you're missing valuable information.

Forgetting to Nurture Leads

Just because a lead isn't ready to buy today doesn't mean they won't be in the future. Too many salespeople let cold leads fall off the radar completely. Instead, keep them in a nurturing sequence—sending them relevant content, checking in periodically, and staying top of mind.

A lead that goes cold now could turn into a warm prospect later. Don't lose track of them.

Final Thoughts
The Heart of B2B Sales

At the end of the day, B2B sales is about more than transactions, figures, or quotas—it's about people. It's about understanding the challenges your customers face, the goals they strive for, and the pressures they navigate daily. It's about positioning yourself not just as a salesperson, but as a partner—someone who helps them find solutions and makes their job easier, their business better.

The strategies and tools in this guide are designed to give you structure, yes. But the real magic happens when you take these concepts and make them your own. When you approach each client conversation with curiosity, when you listen more than you talk, when you treat the sales process as an opportunity to build trust and add value—that's when everything changes.

B2B sales, at its core, is about creating connections. And connections aren't built through clever pitches or perfectly rehearsed presentations. They're built through empathy, through genuine interest, through showing up as someone who cares about the other side of the table.

So here's the takeaway: Selling isn't about being slick or pushy. It's about being human. It's about understanding that behind every deal is a relationship, and behind every relationship is a person who needs to know they can trust you.

Take these principles, put them into action, and watch how your approach to sales evolves. Not every deal will close, and not every conversation will go as planned. But when you approach each interaction with authenticity, when you focus on helping your clients achieve *their* goals, you'll find that the sales will follow naturally.

As you continue your journey in B2B sales, keep this in mind: success isn't measured only by the deals you close, but by the relationships you build along the way. Sales is about trust, value, and service — and if you keep those at the heart of everything you do, the results will speak for themselves.

www.ingramcontent.com/pod-product-compliance
Lightning Source LLC
Chambersburg PA
CBHW070304220526
45465CB00004B/1744